Introduction

About this guide

This guide is written for students following the OCR A2 Critical Thinking course. It deals with Unit F503 (Unit 3): Ethical Reasoning and Decision Making.

It is not intended to be a comprehensive and detailed set of notes; you will need to supplement this material with further reading.

The guide is divided into three sections:

- This **Introduction** provides an outline of the demands of the unit, the format of the exam paper and the skills required to complete the unit successfully. There is also some general guidance on preparing for the examination.
- The **Content Guidance** section introduces the key skills required for Unit F503, in the order in which they will be used in the examination. It also includes a brief introduction to ethical principles with which candidates should be familiar.
- The **Questions and Answers** section includes a sample Unit F503 resource booklet and a sample question paper. Advice is included to help you tackle the questions successfully. Sample A-grade and C-grade responses are provided, together with examiner comments.

Unit F503

At AS, you should have been introduced to **principles**, which are general rule-like statements that can be applied to a number of different issues. Unit F503 takes this further by introducing you to **moral principles** and **ethical reasoning**.

There is more content in Unit F503 than in the other critical thinking units because you are expected to be aware of some ethical theories. If you are also studying subjects such as philosophy and ethics, you may already be familiar with these theories. However, you will not necessarily be at an advantage and you need to be aware that this unit is *not* intended to be a general course in ethics. Candidates who simply repeat the theories of dead eighteenth-century philosophers are unlikely to achieve a good grade.

This unit is about the application of principles — which may or may not be based on ethical theories — to a controversial issue. This issue will be introduced in the resource booklet (see p. 47). Examples of issues include:

- responses to terrorism
- designer babies
- wind farms
- animal testing
- identity cards
- the arms trade

Whatever the issue, there will be a **moral dimension**. The reasoning will be about what we *ought* to do in relation to dilemmas that arise from the issue.

Resource booklet

The resource booklet forms part of the exam paper. It contains several short documents to introduce the issue. Prior knowledge of the issue is not required.

You should read the documents carefully and *think critically* about the evidence they contain. They may include definitions, factual data, opinions and arguments, numerical data, tables, graphs and/or charts.

You will be expected to analyse and evaluate the conflicting ideas and arguments within this range of source material.

Skills

You should read the resource booklet critically. You will be expected to be aware of problems with the source material, such as:
- whether the views expressed may have been influenced by factors such as religious beliefs or political opinions
- the extent to which the credibility of evidence is strengthened or weakened by such factors as bias and vested interest
- the extent to which statistical evidence is reliable
- the extent to which key words and terms have problems of definition, such as ambiguity and vagueness

You will also be expected to identify a range of **criteria**, such as cost, public opinion and effectiveness, which might be useful in making decisions from a range of **choices**.

Having identified a range of choices, you must be able to identify a **dilemma**. Successful candidates will show that, where there is a dilemma, there are undesirable consequences that arise from each available choice.

You will then have to construct an **argument** that seeks to resolve the dilemma by:
- identifying relevant principles
- evaluating these principles
- making critical references to the source documents

Preparing for the examination

You need to be aware of a range of principles that can be applied to the ethical issues presented in the resource booklet. Some ethical principles are outlined in the following section of this guide.

Contents

Introduction

■ ■ ■

Content Guidance

■ ■ ■

Questions and Answers

Remember that you are not expected to describe the ethical theories at length. The focus is on *identifying* principles and then *applying* them to the issues arising from the material in the resource booklet. You must also be able to recognise the strengths and limitations of these principles.

Beyond familiarising yourself with these theories, it is unlikely that you will spend a great deal of time revising for this or any other critical thinking unit. It would be more useful and interesting to develop your knowledge and understanding of ethical issues that arise in the media as a result of current controversies. It is essential to read a quality newspaper such as *The Times*, the *Daily Telegraph*, the *Guardian* or the *Independent* every day.

Listening to the arguments of others is also good preparation for this examination and beneficial to your A-level studies in general. Programmes such as the *Today* programme, *Any Questions?* and the *Moral Maze* on Radio 4 are highly recommended and you can listen for free, and at any time, on the BBC's iPlayer.

The examination

The examination lasts for 90 minutes, and you must answer *all* the questions on the paper. It is marked out of 60, and comprises 25% of the total A-level marks.

Many candidates worry about running out of time, and therefore want to start writing straight away. However, it is unlikely that any candidate can be successful in this unit without spending at least 10 minutes reading the resource booklet carefully before putting pen to paper.

As you read the documents in the resource booklet, think critically about the claims being made, the use and misuse of evidence, the credibility of the evidence offered and any problems of definition that arise. It is a good idea to write some notes on the documents for later use. Making critical comments in your answer about specific documents that are clearly referenced will usually lead to high marks.

The exam paper is likely to start with some introductory questions. On the specimen paper, these are worth only 4 marks each, so you should not need to spend too long answering them — about 5 minutes per question is adequate.

A more important question (20 marks on the specimen paper) asks you to explain how the *choices* that we could make are affected by the *criteria* that are used. You should spend around 30 minutes tackling this question.

The final question carries the highest number of marks. You should spend around 40 minutes writing a dilemma and then developing a reasoned argument that seeks to resolve it.

Content Guidance

T here are three chapters in this section, each of which relates to the questions likely to arise on the examination paper.

(1) Source documents

This chapter looks at the introductory questions, which deal with interpreting the material in the resource booklet.

(2) Choices, criteria and dilemmas

This chapter deals with the skills required for tackling the 'criteria and choices' question on the paper and with the dilemmas that might arise.

(3) Ethical principles

This chapter introduces some important ethical principles that may be useful in tackling the final question on the paper, which requires you to use such principles to try to resolve the dilemma.

Introduction to the bin collection issue

Every F503 paper will focus on a controversial issue that has ethical implications. This guide will focus on the issue of bin collections.

Until the 1980s, the service provided by dustmen was to collect metal dustbins, often from the rear of houses or wherever people happened to keep their bins. Binmen would enter your property to collect your rubbish and then replace the bin.

From the 1980s onwards, the level of service deteriorated as local councils strove to make the service more cost-efficient. It became common for householders to be required to take their own bins out to specified positions at the kerbside in black bags or 'wheelie-bins'. Many councils also started charging additional fees for the collection of some items.

More recently, the focus has been on reducing the amount of rubbish sent to landfill sites by encouraging householders to recycle. The government, apparently motivated by targets set by the European Union's 'Landfill Directive', has put pressure on local councils to collect less rubbish by fining them for exceeding their landfill quotas. Many councils have switched to fortnightly refuse collections, which are officially known as AWCs (alternate weekly collections). These have been unpopular with some residents, especially with older people who remember the service that used to be provided by the traditional British dustman.

Source documents

The introductory questions on the exam paper may ask you to:
- consider problems arising from certain documents in the resource booklet
- identify factors that may affect people's views
- identify problems that exist in the definition of key words or terms

Problems arising from the documents

The first thing you should do in the examination is read the resource booklet, which will contain a number of documents providing information about a controversial issue. The information may or may not be reliable — and it would obviously be unwise to rely on unreliable information when making an important decision.

Problems in the documents could arise from:
- bias
- vested interests
- irrelevant expertise
- unreliable statistics

Bias

A biased document is likely to have less credibility than a balanced one. Bias could exist in a document if it presents a one-sided case. Sometimes an author acknowledges only one side of the argument, ignoring alternative points of view; or the writer may present evidence in such a way as to make it appear that only one conclusion can be drawn from it, disregarding the possibility of alternative explanations.

Bias exists on both sides of the rubbish collection issue. To illustrate this point, it might be useful briefly to consider the increase in rat populations that some people contend has been caused, or at least made much worse, by less frequent refuse collections.

A website called the 'Campaign for Weekly Waste Collection' (**www.weeklywaste.com**) draws attention to health risks associated with mice, rats, maggots and flies that can be attracted to uncollected rubbish. It concludes: 'We should act before we have an insurmountable pest problem leading to a 21st century plague.'

In 2006, the *Daily Mail* ran a 'campaign to save weekly rubbish collections'. In the following example, it explores the issue of rats.

> ### Dawn of the super rat
>
> Martin Delgado in the *Daily Mail* (16 September 2006) reported warnings from vermin control experts that the demise of weekly rubbish collections 'has helped to create a new breed of super rat'.
>
> One 'scientist' said, 'Rats are becoming more intelligent. It's almost as if they are one step ahead of us.'

Readers of such articles might be given the impression that the rat population has increased because of alternate weekly rubbish collections. However, just because there may be a correlation between increased rat populations and alternate weekly rubbish collection, it does not automatically follow that the new collection systems have *caused* the increased number of rats.

It is important to consider what alternative explanations there may be for the extra rats. Popular suggestions are a succession of mild winters (providing better breeding conditions for rats), growth in the number of derelict properties and an increase in litter (especially in the form of half-eaten takeaway food). Less obvious is the fact that some apparently environmentally-friendly activities can encourage rats. For example, rats can be attracted to residential properties by bird feeders and by the composting of food waste.

This does not prove that the new rubbish collection systems have not encouraged rats. After all, if rat populations are increasing, for whatever reason, it could be argued that the collection of waste, especially of food waste, should be as frequent as possible to avoid encouraging them still further. Nevertheless, the important point, for the present purpose, is to observe that a document can be said to be biased if it is claiming that alternate weekly rubbish collection is responsible for the explosion in the rat population, without acknowledging that there are alternative explanations.

Vested interests

Vested interests can weaken the credibility of documents because they provide a motive to misrepresent the truth. It is important to examine the source material closely and to ask who wrote the documents and why.

Authors may have a motive to misrepresent the truth if they have something to gain or something to lose from the outcome of an issue. For example, politicians are often motivated by the need to achieve popularity, to win votes and secure re-election. So, a politician could sometimes be tempted to support a position just because of its popularity.

So why would a politician want to support an *unpopular* policy? It could be that the vested interest is not as obvious as it first appears. For example, a local councillor might support the 'unpopular' rubbish collection system because the alternative could be higher council tax, as the council would be fined if it did not cut the amount of rubbish sent to landfill sites. He or she could be calculating that increases in council tax would prove even more unpopular than a new rubbish collection system and so might be choosing what he or she sees as the lesser of two evils.

On the other hand, it is important not to be too cynical. Just because people have a motive to lie, it does not automatically follow that they *will* lie. A more charitable interpretation would be that many local councillors are genuinely convinced by the environmental benefits of the new rubbish collection systems and that they support them out of principle and in spite of their unpopularity.

Common error

Students frequently struggle to see the difference between bias and vested interests:

- In a biased document, the information is presented in an unbalanced way, often ignoring common counter-arguments.
- A vested interest exists where there is something to be lost or gained through the outcome of the dispute, resulting in there being a motive to misrepresent the truth.

Do not be tempted to say, 'This document is biased because the author has a vested interest'. Such an answer would be inadequate because a document is not necessarily biased just because the author has a vested interest. In any case, it would be necessary to explain the nature of the vested interest by showing that the author had a motive to misrepresent the truth.

A vested interest *can* lead to bias, but bias does not necessarily have to result from a vested interest. Consider the manager of a football team who challenges every refereeing decision that goes against his side. His bias results from the vested interest that he has in his team winning the match. His vested interest could be in avoiding the sack and it results in his biased outlook. However, his team's supporters may also be challenging the same decisions because they are similarly biased; however, their bias does not necessarily result from a vested interest, since supporters do not get the sack if their team loses.

Irrelevant expertise

In scrutinising the authorship of a document, it is useful to look for evidence of relevant expertise. A document could lack credibility if technical information is presented by people who lack the qualifications to make such judgements.

If qualifications or expertise are cited, it is important to consider their relevance to the issue, in order to avoid the 'irrelevant appeal to authority'.

The Campaign for Weekly Waste Collection website is written by Doretta Cocks, BSc (Environmental Sciences). The credibility of her claims about rats and public health is increased because of the apparent relevance of her academic qualification.

In other documents, problems can occur where there is a lack of evidence of expertise or a suggestion that the authority may not be entirely relevant. Consider the following example:

Rotting kitchen waste

Claims that fortnightly rubbish collections do not pose a health risk have been shot down by waste experts.

Senior rubbish collection officials told a committee of MPs yesterday that rotting kitchen waste must be collected once a week in the interests of public health.

Source: extract from an article by Jane Merrick, the *Daily Mail* (22 May 2007)

content guidance

What is a 'waste expert'? Is this a person who understands how waste is collected or someone who understands the health implications of leaving waste uncollected? Would a 'rubbish collection official' involved in the collection and disposal of refuse necessarily be a reliable authority on the spread of disease? If not, the expertise of the 'senior rubbish collection officials' may be *irrelevant* to the issue of health risks.

Unreliable statistics

Alternate weekly rubbish collections are popular with some people but unpopular with others. To determine the overall popularity or unpopularity of the new system, some sort of opinion poll would be required.

In an opinion poll, it is not necessary to ask everyone what they think, because a sample (often fewer than 1,000 people) can be accurate in representing the opinion of the entire population. However, it is important to ensure that the sample is unbiased and that the questions are selected carefully.

A famous example of a biased sample is that used by the *Literary Digest* (**http://en.wikipedia.org/wiki/Opinion_poll**) in attempting to predict the outcome of the 1936 US presidential election. The sample of 2.3 million voters was huge but it was not scientifically selected and the people who responded tended to be wealthier Americans. The publication relied on a telephone poll, which was conducted at a time when only richer people owned telephones. Consequently, the *Literary Digest* failed to predict the correct outcome of the election.

Website surveys and phone-in polls can produce notoriously unreliable results because the sample is self-selected. The following example is from a local newspaper in Peterborough:

90% want weekly collections

The *Peterborough Evening Telegraph* (29 September 2005) ran a readers' poll to ask the public if the city council should revert to weekly bin collections. Of the 1,668 readers who took part in the poll, 90% supported weekly black bin collections.

The problem with this survey is that only readers of the *Peterborough Evening Telegraph* were included in the poll and it was a self-selecting sample. The 1,668 people who took part would probably not be representative of public opinion on this issue.

Opposition to alternate weekly collections is clear from this report of 'raging residents' in Lancashire:

Bin rage

The *Lancashire Evening Post* (10 June 2005) reported that, 'Raging residents are attacking Preston's army of binmen'.

> Anger erupted after new bin-collection systems were introduced by the local council. 'Refuse collectors have been forced to flee many of Preston's estates after coming under a barrage of abuse from angry householders. In some cases, bags of rubbish have been thrown at the dust wagons.'

It would be unwise to draw too many conclusions from this report, however. There would be a danger in drawing a hasty generalisation from what may be a localised phenomenon. Unless we can find similar examples of 'raging residents' from elsewhere in the UK, it could be that there were particular problems in Preston that were unrepresentative of the country as a whole.

A significant problem in gauging public opinion on this issue lies in the contradictions that can emerge from a detailed survey of public opinion. This was illustrated in an episode of *The Simpsons*, in which Homer became Springfield's Sanitation Commissioner and discovered that a comprehensive rubbish collection service was popular but that the accompanying high local taxes and environmental damage were even more unpopular (**http://en.wikipedia.org/wiki/Trash_of_the_Titans**). As previously stated, many local councils may be calculating that council tax increases caused by penalty fees for exceeding landfill quotas would be more unpopular than the restrictive collection systems.

Problems with documents: examination tips

When considering problems that might arise from a given document, ask yourself these questions:
- Is there evidence of bias (or neutrality)?
- What do we know about the expertise of the author?
- Is the author an expert and, if so, is the expertise relevant to the issue?
- Could there be a vested interest to misrepresent the truth?
- Are there weaknesses in the use of statistics?
- Is the information out of date?

To achieve good marks:
- Explain the problem fully.
- Explain the *significance* of the problem.

Factors affecting views

In a typical exam question, you might be referred to one or two of the documents and asked to identify and explain factors that might affect how people react to the issue.

The specification recommends that you consider social, political, religious and moral factors. However, you do not need to consider all of these categories on each paper. In considering the issue of refuse collection, social and political factors are likely to be the most important.

An example of a social factor could be the risk of social unrest and crime. The following report from a local paper in Cannock suggests that bin-related crime can be caused by the new collection systems.

> ### Recycling scheme sparks bin thefts
>
> Panicking families are stealing neighbours' wheelie bins after dark to cope with the rubbish loads they produce since the council's controversial recycling scheme swung into action.
>
> Fearing that their own bins are not enough to cope with the fortnight's rubbish produced between collections, law-abiding neighbours are turning into law-breakers and stealing those in other gardens.
>
> 'It's like something out of Mad Max,' said unemployed Paul Nicholls, 42, from Great Wyrley.
>
> Source: extract from an article by Mike Bradley, the *Cannock Chase Post* (27 June 2005)

Social unrest on housing estates may be a localised issue, but it has also been widely suggested that alternate weekly collection could lead to an increase in the illegal dumping of rubbish, known as 'fly tipping'. A desire to avoid such negative social outcomes might be a factor affecting people's views on the rubbish collection issue.

Other relevant social factors could be the size of the household and the nature of the housing. A large family generally produces more rubbish than a single person and may struggle to fit its general waste into a single bin. A person living alone, by contrast, might be in favour of a 'pay as you throw' scheme, if this would result in a lower tax rate for those who throw away less rubbish.

The nature of the housing has been an issue for some people who live in blocks of flats where there are communal bins. Some residents may be more careful than others in wrapping and disposing of their waste, and there could be serious problems of smell, especially in the warmer months. A person living in such housing might be expected to be in favour of more frequent rubbish collection, particularly in the summer.

Typical examination question

Refer to Documents 1 and 3. Identify and explain three factors that might affect how people react to the issue of refuse collection systems. (4 marks)

Marks would be awarded for identifying the factors, explaining their relevance and making specific reference to Documents 1 and 3. Answers should be brief. It should be possible to achieve maximum marks by writing only five or six lines.

Problems of definition

The F503 paper will often ask you to identify why a certain key word or phrase has problems of definition. Even if this question is not asked directly, it is important that key words and terms are clearly defined in the extended argument at the end of the examination.

Some problems of definition occur because of **ambiguity** in the language. According to Jeff Gray (**www.gray-area.org/Research/Ambig**), the 500 most frequently used words in the English language have an average of 23 different meanings. The word 'round', for example, has 70 distinctly different meanings.

Sometimes problems of ambiguity occur because of how a word is placed in a sentence, or because of a lack of punctuation. Over the years, this has led to some amusing examples, especially in newspaper headlines such as 'Sikh Girl Wins Trouser Case' and, on the eve of US president George Bush's visit to the UK in 2003, 'Giant Police Exercise To Guard Bush' (BBC Ceefax, 2003).

The Hitchhiker's Guide to the Galaxy

Ford Prefect: 'You better be prepared for the jump into hyperspace. It's unpleasantly like being drunk.'

Arthur Dent: 'What's so unpleasant about being drunk?'

Ford Prefect: 'You ask a glass of water.'

Source: extract from Adams, D. (1979) *The Hitchhiker's Guide to the Galaxy*

In the examination, the problems of definition are likely to be somewhat less obvious; problems of ambiguity are, nevertheless, common. Whenever a word or term can be interpreted differently, it is important that you define, at the outset of an argument, exactly what meaning you are intending to use.

Below are some examples to illustrate problems of definition.

Poverty

Most people have a vague understanding of what poverty means and most would agree that poverty is a bad thing. In 1997, the new UK Labour government announced that 35% of British children lived in poverty. Many people found this announcement quite surprising, given that Britain is such a rich country. Jamie Whyte (*Bad Thoughts*, 2003) observes that the poorest people in Britain are the unemployed, who receive free housing, free medical care, free education and cash sums to pay for other necessities. Most of the poorest people in Britain own televisions, cars, stereos and telephones. How could 35% of British children be living in poverty? The answer is in Labour's definition of poverty, which has nothing to do with a lack of access to food, healthcare, education, housing, or even television sets and mobile phones. Labour defined 'poverty' as living in a household where the income is less than 60% of the national median. Whyte observes that, under Labour's definition, it would be possible to take a family out of poverty by lowering their income, as long as the income of the rich was lowered even more. If Britain became a poorer country, there might actually be fewer children living in poverty.

The government was using a **relative** rather than an **absolute** definition of poverty, in which people can be said to be living below the poverty line if they do not have access to those things that the majority of people in their society take for granted. Such poverty will not be eliminated by the society becoming richer; it will be eliminated only by the society becoming more equal, with a narrower gap between the 'haves' and the 'have-nots'. The relative definition of poverty emphasises the *context* in determining whether or not a person can be said to be living in poverty. Someone is poor when he or she has a level of income much lower than that of most other people in society. Such a person may lack the resources to participate in activities and to have living conditions that are expected and encouraged in the local community.

Health

The World Health Organization (WHO) defines health as 'a state of complete physical, mental and social wellbeing and not merely the absence of disease or infirmity'.

In the *British Medical Journal*, Rodolfo Saracci argues that there are several problems with this definition (**www.bmj.com/cgi/content/full/314/7091/1409**), for example with situations where mental wellbeing and physical wellbeing come into conflict. A lifestyle involving smoking, drinking alcohol, consuming lots of fatty food and taking no exercise could lead to good *mental* health while being damaging to *physical* health. Saracci quotes Sigmund Freud who, after giving up cigars, commented: 'I learned that health was to be had at a certain cost... Thus I am now better than I was, but not happier.'

Another problem arises if health is seen as a social right. Mary Robinson, in her role as head of the WHO, claimed that we have a human 'right to be healthy' (Whyte, J. in *Bad Thoughts*, 2003), and many other commentators have agreed that health is a human rights issue. Under the WHO's own definition of health, does this mean that the government has a responsibility to ensure that we are happy? As Saracci observes: 'This undervalues personal autonomy and could be established only in totalitarian regimes.'

The environment

In the case of refuse collection systems, there is a problem over what is meant by the term 'the environment'. Both sides in this dispute have claimed that their favoured method of rubbish collection is 'environmentally friendly'. Supporters of the new collection system claim that their motive is to reduce landfill and increase recycling, believing that landfill is environmentally damaging and that recycling is environmentally friendly. Their focus is on the depletion of natural resources and the emission of greenhouse gases.

Opponents of the new rubbish collection system concentrate on problems of smell, fly tipping and rats, which also affect the environment. From their point of view, a measure that results in malodorous rubbish tips and an increase in rodents cannot be said to be good for the environment.

Therefore, when one side of the argument claims to be 'caring for the environment', it is worth questioning *which* aspect(s) of the environment it is referring to.

Problems of definition: examination tips and examples

Think about problems of:
- ambiguity
- vagueness
- context

You should state the problem, explain it clearly, and refer to the documents.

The government's definition of poverty is neither ambiguous nor vague. However, when government ministers talk about 'poverty', they rarely stop to explain that they are using a relative rather than an absolute definition of the word, and this could lead to an audience being misled. The government's definition relies on the context of our modern society in which, for example, the issue of starvation has been replaced with issues of social exclusion and the effects of the 'digital divide'.

The WHO's definition of 'health' is both ambiguous and vague, and it also has some issues of context. Indeed, the definition is so wide that many activities could be seen as both healthy and unhealthy at the same time. If an activity were to be described as 'unhealthy', we would have to consider carefully the type of health that we would be referring to. Furthermore, an activity that might be healthy for one person may be unhealthy for another, depending on age, gender, allergies and many other factors.

Choices, criteria and dilemmas

To tackle questions on this part of the exam paper, you will have to identify:
- a range of choices
- criteria that may be applied in assessing the choices
- a dilemma that arises from the problem

The sixth-form kitchen

In a school, the sixth formers have the privilege of using a kitchen, but there is a long-running problem of a minority of sixth-form students failing to clean up after themselves. This causes annoyance and inconvenience to domestic staff, teaching staff and other sixth formers. No one ever knows who is responsible for the mess, so whenever the issue is raised, it is simply said that 'something must be done'.

It is easy enough to say that 'something must be done', but further consideration is needed to come up with a range of choices. Faced with this problem, two critical-thinking students, Kimberley Bannister and Francesca Sharp ('The More's Kitchen Fiasco', 2005), came up with the following 'continuum of choice':

- Do nothing and tolerate the mess.
- Display notices requesting that people clean up after themselves.
- Call a house assembly and make an emotional appeal.
- Remove kitchen privileges for all students as a 'blanket punishment'.
- Install a CCTV system to detect the offenders.
- Adopt a combination of armed security guards and a 'shoot-to-kill' policy.

If we are going to develop a policy for responding to the problem of mess in the sixth-form kitchen, we need **criteria** that can be used to make choices. Such criteria could be:

- cost
- effectiveness
- human rights

It can be seen that these criteria come into conflict. For example, putting up notices is a cheap response, as notices are inexpensive. However, the notices are unlikely to be effective, because the selfish minority that causes the mess may simply ignore them.

Another conflict is that the more effective responses would lead to problems with 'rights'. For example, removing kitchen privileges by locking the kitchen as a 'blanket punishment' could be effective (at least in the short term), but some sixth formers may feel that their 'rights' are being violated, especially since the innocent are suffering as a result of the misdemeanours of the true culprits. They may also feel that a right to privacy would be violated by a CCTV system, and the right to life and a fair trial would be violated by a 'shoot-to-kill' policy. The concept of 'rights', what they are and where they come from, is an issue for further discussion in the next section of this guide; for present purposes, it is sufficient to establish that a shoot-to-kill policy would certainly be effective because few sixth formers would risk death to avoid doing the washing-up, but the school would run into serious legal problems if they started shooting their sixth formers.

The more effective choices seem to be the more costly ones. CCTV might be an effective deterrent but it would be expensive to install. Armed security guards would be even more costly to employ, and this is before we consider the legal issues that might arise if the armed guards ever actually used their weapons.

Identifying a dilemma

Thus we can see that **dilemmas** arise where there is a difficult choice to be made, with negative consequences arising from each choice. The word 'dilemma' comes from the Greek *di lemma*, meaning 'two propositions'. The phrase 'wrestling with the horns of a dilemma' invites us to imagine facing an angry bull and to consider which horn we would rather be impaled with. That is rather like being asked whether you would prefer to be hanged or shot, in that each option is, in some way, undesirable.

A dilemma is a difficult choice with harm on both sides. A problem such as 'What should I have for pudding?' is not a dilemma, because the choices are not clearly explained. 'Should I have treacle tart or fruit salad?' is not a dilemma either, because the choice is not unpleasant; there is no obvious harm from either option. When expressing a dilemma, remember to be clear what the choice is and what negative consequences arise from each option.

Typical examination question

State and explain a dilemma that arises from making decisions about the sixth-form kitchen.   (2 marks)

'What should they do about the mess in the sixth form kitchen?' is not a dilemma. It is a vague question with no explanation of the harm on either side.

'Should we put up notices asking people to clear up after themselves, or should we install a CCTV system to detect the true offenders?' would attract half marks. Choices have been made clear, but the negative consequences arising from each course of action have not been explained.

'Should we have a policy of putting up notices, which would be cheap but may be ineffective, or should we have a CCTV system, which could be effective but would cost a lot of money?' is a much better answer, because it clearly explains that there are drawbacks arising from either choice.

Ethical principles

An **ethical** issue is one where there is a question as to what *ought* to be done. Ethical questions have a **moral** dimension, dealing with issues of right and wrong.

Not all rules or laws are based on moral principles. Killing and stealing are generally both illegal and immoral. However, morality goes further than the law: no legal system can outlaw all immoral behaviour, such as lying, cheating or being unkind to others. There may also be some examples of laws that are immoral, having been imposed by corrupt or evil regimes. Therefore, a legal act is not necessarily moral, and acting morally does not always involve acting legally.

Moral behaviour is not necessarily doing what most people do. 'When in Rome, do as the Romans do' is not a reliable guide to moral behaviour, because different cultures have different moral standards, and what people do is not necessarily what they *ought* to do. In ancient Rome, for example, slavery was socially acceptable.

Morality cannot be based only on feelings. Just because something makes you feel guilty, it does not automatically follow that your behaviour was immoral. Furthermore, just because you feel good, it does not automatically follow that you have done nothing wrong.

Nor can morality be based entirely on religion. Many people do not have a religion but they can still behave morally. Some religions have detailed moral codes that can encourage moral behaviour but there may still be some issues where it would be difficult to see how religious teaching could be applied.

Distinguishing between *is* and *ought*

Ethics is concerned not with what *is* the case but with what *ought to be* the case. It is to do with how the world *ought* to be and how people *ought* to conduct themselves.

Generally, it is difficult to argue from 'what *is*' to 'what *ought to be*' without making an error of reasoning. For example: 'Yes, I am jealous of her but there's nothing wrong with being jealous because jealousy is only natural.' The problem with this reasoning is that, just because human beings may be jealous creatures, it does not necessarily follow that they *ought* to be jealous.

Principles

A **principle** is a general rule that can be applied in various situations. When resolving dilemmas, most of us will, consciously or otherwise, rely on some principles to help in the decision-making process.

Boxing in schools

Boxing should not be taught in schools because it is a violent and dangerous sport and schools should not be encouraging violent or dangerous activities.

In the above example, in order to decide whether or not schools should teach boxing, the author has relied on a principle that schools should not be teaching violent or dangerous activities.

If the author is to be consistent with his principle, we would expect him also to be opposed to other dangerous or violent sports in schools, such as rugby. If the author was against boxing but in favour of rugby, he could be accused of being inconsistent with his principle. This illustrates the importance of thinking carefully before establishing principles; remember that principles always have a wider application.

General principles exercise

Read the following arguments and consider:
(1) What is the general principle that is stated or implied by the author?
(2) If the author is to be consistent, what other conclusions would he or she need to support?

> **Argument A**
>
> 'Homosexual marriage should not be allowed because the Bible says that homosexuality is a sin.'
>
> **Argument B**
>
> 'Smokers should not be treated on the NHS if their illnesses are self-inflicted.'
>
> **Argument C**
>
> 'Britain should not trade with Zimbabwe because that country has a bad human rights record.'

In Argument A, the principle is that a law that conflicts with the Bible is wrong. To be consistent, the author would have to accept that other things that are outlawed by the Bible should also be illegal. For example, in 1 Corinthians 4:33–35, St Paul seems to establish a rule that women should remain silent in church. If she wants to inquire about something, a woman should wait until she gets home and then ask her husband. If the law is to be based entirely on biblical rules, other seemingly undesirable activities may need to be legalised. For example, in Exodus 21:7, it is suggested that a father is allowed to sell his daughter into slavery if he needs to repay a debt.

In Argument B, the principle is that people should not get treatment on the NHS if their illness is self-inflicted. To be consistent, the author might also want to prevent other groups of people from receiving treatment, for example alcoholics, drug addicts, obese people, those who engage in dangerous sports and reckless drivers.

In Argument C, the principle is that Britain should not trade with countries that have a bad human rights record. To be consistent, the author would presumably want Britain to cease trading with other countries that have a bad human rights record, such as China and Saudi Arabia.

In the examination, you will be expected to use principles to resolve a dilemma. Because the issue will have a moral dimension, it is likely that some of the principles used will be ethical.

Ethical theories try to make sense of the fundamental question of how we can tell what is right and what is wrong.

Learning and Careers

Moral relativism

When you make an argument in favour of a particular position, do you find that some people respond by saying, 'well, that's just your opinion'? Why do people say this? It seems to be nothing more than a statement of the obvious and completely inadequate as a counter-argument.

What seems to underlie this is a modern trend towards **relativism**, that holds that one person's opinion, especially on a moral issue, cannot be any better than someone else's opinion. This is all very polite and non-confrontational and tolerant of differences, but the problem is that most people would want to take this principle only so far. There comes a point at which most of us would concede that the difference between right and wrong cannot be just a matter of personal opinion.

Different people have different opinions and feelings, and so they disagree. Just because we each have the right to hold differing opinions, it does not follow that we all have to be right.

If one person believes that torture, in some circumstances, is right because it can make dangerous and guilty people confess, and someone else believes that torture is always wrong, can it follow that both these people are right? The important issue of whether or not torture can be justified surely cannot be settled simply by accepting that different people have different preferences.

If personal preference, feelings or opinions are not the basis of morality, it follows that there are some things that are *objectively* right or wrong. In other words, if torture is wrong, then it is wrong whether or not you agree that it is wrong. You may have the right to hold a dissenting opinion but your opinion would be mistaken or misguided.

Many people have a problem with this because they understand that some things can be proven more easily than others. People would tend to agree that the world is round because strong scientific evidence exists to demonstrate that this is a fact. Answers to moral questions cannot be proved scientifically; however, ethical theories have been devised, which are attempts to provide a system for showing which things are right and which are wrong.

> A student in an ethics class announced that she was a relativist. The professor responded, 'That's fine, however, I'm going to give you an F in this course as a result.' The student protested: 'But, that's not fair!' 'Oh, really?' replied the professor. 'I thought you were a relativist. Do you mean to tell me you think that there really is a standard of fairness? Tell me about it.'
>
> Source: http://paulsjusticepage.com/cjethics/intro/relativism.htm

Cultural relativism

Cultural relativism is the view that the concepts of right and wrong arise from cultural beliefs and that we should be tolerant of differences between cultures. For example, it is common in many cultures for men to be allowed to take more than one wife. In cultures that allow polygamy, the practice is respectable and even encouraged, although it is outlawed in other societies. If we think polygamy is wrong but other cultures hold that it is right, are we in a position to judge the moral standards of another culture?

There have been many situations where one culture has tried to impose its moral standards on another by either force or persuasion. For example, people in Western cultures were outraged by the treatment of women in Afghanistan, which was ruled by the Taliban from 1996 to 2001. The Taliban imposed a strict interpretation of Islamic sharia law, under which women were not allowed to be educated after the age of eight. Women seeking an education had to study in underground schools, and they and their teachers risked execution if caught. Women were not allowed to be examined by male doctors, which led to illnesses remaining untreated. Women violating these and other strict laws were flogged in the streets or executed (**http://en.wikipedia.org/wiki/Taliban**).

The Taliban could, and did, argue that their rules were based on their interpretation of Islamic law and that they were entitled to their point of view. Their idea of right and wrong came from their culture and they argued that it was arrogant Western imperialism to suggest that an alternative culture was superior. Nevertheless, even though most of the people being oppressed by the Taliban came from the same culture and shared the same religion, they had a different idea of morality. If we accept cultural relativism, whose side should we be on?

A further example is that, 200 years ago, slavery was common in many societies and cultures. Owning another human being was respectable and moral, yet nowadays the idea causes outrage. Our moral values have changed and most people would want to argue that they have changed for the better. Can it be that something that was once right has now become wrong, or is it the case that slavery has always been wrong and that it is only recently that we have come to realise that it was wrong?

Confusing *is* and *ought*

Just because a particular behaviour *is* commonly accepted, it does not automatically follow that it *ought to be* commonly accepted.

Slavery came to be abolished because an initially small group of people argued that what was normal in their culture should no longer be considered acceptable. Something is not right just because it is what most people do or what most people think.

Cultural relativism is appealing because it appears to be tolerant of cultural differences. However, it is difficult to defend the idea that what is moral is whatever a culture happens to think is moral at a particular point in time.

Utilitarianism

Utilitarianism is not a relativist position; it asserts that right or wrong is not just a matter of personal preference, since it is possible to work out objectively the rightness or wrongness of possible courses of action. However, what utilitarians and relativists have in common is that they would agree that nothing is right or wrong in each and every situation. They would agree, in other words, that right and wrong are not absolutes.

For utilitarians, what matters is the consequence of an action rather than the act itself. In order to work out what is right, people should consider the situation carefully and calculate what course of action would result in the greatest happiness for the greatest number.

Bernard Williams offers the following dilemma as an example of a situation in which many people would be tempted to adopt utilitarian reasoning:

Jim and the Indians

Jim finds himself in the central square of a small South American town. Tied up against the wall are a row of twenty Indians, most terrified, a few defiant, in front of them several armed men in uniform. A heavy man in a sweat-stained khaki shirt turns out to be the captain in charge and, after a good deal of questioning of Jim that establishes that he got there by accident while on a botanical expedition, explains that the Indians are a random group of the inhabitants who, after recent acts of protest against the government, are just about to be killed to remind other possible protestors of the advantages of not protesting. However, since Jim is an honoured visitor from another land, the captain is happy to offer him a guest's privilege of killing one of the Indians himself. If Jim accepts, then as a special mark of the occasion, the other Indians will be let off. If Jim refuses, then there is no special occasion, and Pedro here will do what he was about to do when Jim arrived, and kill them all. Jim, with some desperate recollection of schoolboy fiction, wonders whether if he got hold of a gun, he could hold the captain, Pedro and the rest of the soldiers to threat, but it is quite clear from the set-up that nothing of that kind is going to work: any attempt at that sort of thing will mean that all the Indians will be killed, and himself. The men against the wall, and the other villagers, understand the situation, and are obviously begging him to accept. What should he do?

Source: Williams, B. 'A critique of utilitarianism' in Smart and Williams (1973)
Utilitarianism: For and Against

Killing is generally considered to be wrong and, if killing is wrong in an absolute sense, then Jim would be wrong to kill because there can be no exceptions to the general rule. However, in this situation, many people would say that the right thing for Jim to do is to kill one man to save the 19 others, especially since the one man whom Jim would kill would be killed anyway, and also because the men and the other villagers are begging Jim to accept the offer to do this.

The utilitarian would argue that, in this situation, killing one man would result in the greatest happiness of the greatest number. We can see this by performing a 'happiness calculation'.

Daniel Sokol ('What if?', *BBC Magazine*, 2 May 2007 **http://news.bbc.co.uk/1/hi/magazine/4954856.stm**) presents three further situations in which people may be tempted to use the utilitarian principle.

The runaway trolley car

A runaway trolley car is hurtling down a track. In its path are five people who will definitely be killed unless you, a bystander, flip a switch which will divert it onto another track, where it will kill one person. Should you flip the switch?

This situation may seem a little harder, because killing the one man saves only five lives compared to the 19 that would be saved by Jim and because the one man who would be killed would not die if you did *not* take action. Furthermore, the one man who would be killed by flipping the switch is not begging you to flip it. Nevertheless, most people find this dilemma quite straightforward and would advocate flipping the switch.

The fat man and the trolley car

The runaway trolley car is hurtling down a track where it will kill five people. You are standing on a bridge above the track and, aware of the imminent disaster, you decide to jump on the track to block the trolley car. Although you will die, the five people will be saved. Just before your leap, you realise that you are too light to stop the trolley. Next to you, a fat man is standing on the edge of the bridge. He would certainly block the trolley, although he would undoubtedly die from the impact. A small nudge and he would fall right onto the track below. No one would ever know. Should you push him?

Although most people would advocate flipping the switch in the first situation, only a minority would consider it right to push the fat man off the bridge, but it is difficult to explain why. Is it because the action of pushing a man off a bridge would seem to be a more direct method of killing than flipping a switch? Alternatively, it could be because people are morally inconsistent.

The cave explorers

An enormous rock falls and blocks the exit of a cave you and five other tourists have been exploring. Fortunately, you spot a hole elsewhere and decide to let 'Big Jack' out first. But Big Jack, a man of generous proportions, gets stuck in the hole. He cannot be moved and there is no other way out. The high tide is rising and, unless you get out soon, everyone but Big Jack (whose head is sticking out of the cave) will inevitably drown. Searching through your backpack, you find a stick of dynamite. It will not move the rock, but will certainly blast Big Jack out of the hole. Big Jack, anticipating your thoughts, pleads for his life. He does not want to die, but neither do you and your four companions. Should you blast Big Jack out?

Having rejected the idea of pushing the fat man off the bridge, most people revert to utilitarianism in the third scenario. In both cases, one life can be taken to save a greater number — but a major difference here is that you are one of the people about to die.

These three examples illustrate effectively the extent to which people can be inconsistent in their moral reasoning and the problems that can be associated with utilitarianism.

Criticisms of utilitarianism

Many moral philosophers have concluded that utilitarianism is a convincing answer to the question of how we can decide what is right and what is wrong. However, there are also some powerful criticisms of utilitarianism.

One common objection is that it is impossible to predict with certainty the consequences of actions. Utilitarianism relies on people being able to predict the future, yet often things happen that we do not expect. Furthermore, we cannot be certain about what will make other people happy, so can we really be expected to make accurate happiness calculations?

Utilitarianism seems to assert that everyone's happiness is equally important. However, is the happiness of a sadist really as valuable as that of an altruist (see p. 31)? Can we give extra priority to the happiness of ourselves or our own family? Is it immoral, for example, for parents to look after their own children without making an equal effort for other children?

> ### The ones who walk away from Omelas
>
> Ursula Le Guin's short story, 'The ones who walk away from Omelas' (in *The Wind's Twelve Quarters*, 1974), illustrates the problem of sacrificing the interests of individuals for the greater good. The fictional Omelas is a utopian city of happiness and delight, whose inhabitants are intelligent, cultured and refined. Everything about Omelas is pleasing, except for the secret of its happiness, which is that the good fortune of Omelas requires that an unfortunate child be kept in filth, darkness and misery. All her citizens know of this on coming of age and some of them walk away. The story ends: 'The place they go towards is a place even less imaginable to us than the city of happiness. I cannot describe it at all. It is possible it does not exist. But they seem to know where they are going, the ones who walk away from Omelas.'

Given that utilitarianism advocates the greatest happiness of the greatest number of people, could the principle not be used to justify the exploitation of a minority in order to benefit the majority? Imagine there are six people who will die unless they get an organ transplant, each person needing a different organ. Would it be justified for them to murder one healthy person to harvest the required organs? In this situation, in the case of Omelas and in the case of the fat man who could be pushed off the bridge, the problem seems to be that the rights of an individual are being disregarded.

Duty ethics

Deontological (duty) ethics are often associated with the German philosopher Immanuel Kant (1724–1804) and can be contrasted with utilitarian systems.

Let us return to the case of Jim and the Indians. A utilitarian says that killing one man is the right thing to do because this saves 19 lives. However, if Jim refuses the offer and Pedro kills 20 men, are their deaths Jim's responsibility? Utilitarianism would seem to suggest that Jim is, in some way, responsible because he has not acted to achieve the greatest happiness of the greatest number. Duty ethics, by contrast, would say that Jim has done nothing wrong because it is Pedro, not Jim, who has killed the 20 men. Jim did his duty by refusing to lower himself to the level of the murderer.

Kant's system is based on the principle that human beings should aim to do their duty rather than trying to calculate the consequences of their actions. He believed that morality should be based on reason and that it is possible to work out rationally what our duties should be. Once we have established what our duty is, we should concentrate on doing it without worrying too much about the situation or the likely consequences.

Treating others as mere means

Duty ethics holds that all human beings are of equal moral worth and should be treated with equal respect as persons with aims and purposes of their own.

There are many circumstances in which we may 'use' other people for our own purposes. After all, you are probably 'using' your teachers as a means to passing your exams. This is not a problem to Kant because it is a free arrangement. Your teacher was not forced into the teaching profession and he or she is (probably) getting paid.

The problem arises when we use others as **mere means** to achieving an end in which they have no interest. An example would be pushing the fat man off the bridge to save five other people, or the six people killing a healthy individual to harvest the organs for themselves. In these situations, the interests of one person are sacrificed simply for the benefit of others.

Therefore, in duty ethics, it cannot be right to sacrifice the few for the many.

Universalising actions

How often have you heard a teacher say 'If I let you do that, I'd have to let everyone do it' or 'How would you feel if everyone did that?' The principle seems to be that we should not do something unless we would be happy for the whole world to do the same thing. This is a fairly good expression of duty ethics.

Kant's argument is that we should act in a certain way only if we would be happy for the whole world to act in the same way. In other words, we should try *universalising* a proposed course of action to see if we would be happy with the result. If we would not be happy for everyone else to do what we want to do, we should desist in acting in that way ourselves, otherwise we would be guilty of being morally inconsistent. It would not be rational for there to be one rule for us and another rule for everyone else.

Is it important to keep a promise?

Kant offered several examples, one of which involved a situation in which you can only take out a loan if you promise to repay it. Maybe you are not sure that you can repay the loan, so would it be acceptable to make the promise anyway?

Kant argued that it would only be right to make the promise if you would be happy for the whole world to act in the same way. Would you be happy for there to be a universal moral rule that it is perfectly acceptable to make promises that cannot be kept?

We would not be happy for there to be such a rule because there would be a contradiction. The whole system of human beings making promises to one another would fall apart if people felt that they could make promises without having any intention of keeping them.

Therefore, we can reason our way to the conclusion that it is wrong to make a promise without having an intention of keeping it.

Can we ever take the situation into account? According to Kant's system of universalising, we can see that stealing would generally be wrong because it would be undesirable for there to be a universal law that stealing is acceptable and it would involve a contradiction, in that the whole notion of private property would be rendered meaningless. However, what about a situation in which you want to steal food because you are starving? Kant's answer seems to be that you have to universalise from that situation, i.e. would you be happy for all starving people to be allowed to steal?

Criticisms of duty ethics

People cannot always accurately predict the consequences of their actions but most of the time we can predict with some degree of certainty what will happen as a result of what we do. After all, if the universe was totally random, there would be little point in anyone thinking before they acted. Given that rational beings can make choices to produce advantageous consequences, most people would want others to think about the consequences before acting.

It may be true that having good intentions is what makes a good person but shouldn't our intentions be focused on bringing about positive consequences and on avoiding harm? A major problem of duty ethics is that it leads to absolute moral rules, with the result that we cannot make reasonable exceptions to general rules in extreme situations.

Duty ethics seems to have no system for resolving conflicts between duties, and this could cause real problems in using this theory to resolve dilemmas. What should we do, for example, if we have to lie to avoid breaking a promise?

A further problem is that the majority can often lose out because of the focus on the importance of the individual. In duty ethics, sacrificing the interests of an individual for the greater good cannot be justified because human beings cannot be used as 'mere means'.

A final problem is one that is present in both utilitarianism and duty ethics. Why is it that all human beings have to be of equal value and equal worth? Neither system seems to provide a facility whereby we can give preference to ourselves or our own families in our moral decision making, yet many people do think there is some justice in putting our friends and family first, especially where a parent is protecting a child.

Altruism, egoism and the Golden Rule

Many people associate morality with the principle of **altruism**, which is an unselfish concern for the welfare of others. Pure altruism is giving without counting the cost, without having an obligation of duty or regard for reciprocity. Altruists put other people's interests before their own.

It should be noted that there is a difference between the principle of altruism and the 'Golden Rule', which is that we should treat other people in a way in which we would wish to be treated ourselves ('do as you would be done unto').

Altruism advocates putting other people's interests *before* your own, whereas the Golden Rule is that other people's interests are merely equal to your own. In practice, it is difficult to see how an altruistic society could function, with everyone putting other people's interests before their own. Imagine two people trying to walk through a door and each one wanting to hold the door open for the other!

Altruism may be contrasted with **ethical egoism**, which is the view that human beings *ought* to do what is in one's own self-interest. Ethical egoism does not hold that it is necessarily right to cause suffering for others, since it may actually be in our own interests to help others. Human beings are selfish creatures but also social animals, finding that their own interests lie in functioning as part of a social group. A philosophy may be described as egoistic if it holds that we should act with kindness towards others purely for reasons of self-interest. After all, the idea of acting with regard for the interests of everyone except oneself could actually be seen as irrational, in that it could be damaging and degrading to the self.

Sometimes we regard as ignoble the idea that a person may be acting kindly towards others because of an ultimately selfish motive, but is it really so bad if good deeds are committed from selfish motives and is it really rational or desirable that anyone should act with disregard for their own interests?

The Golden Rule	Love your neighbour as yourself.
Altruism	Put other people's interests before your own.
Egoism	It is right to act according to motives of self-interest.

Libertarianism

Human beings value their freedom, and many people believe that they generally act according to selfish motives (even when doing apparently altruistic things). How is it, then, that human beings have come to live in societies with leaders and rules and in which there is a significant absence of personal liberty?

Thomas Hobbes (1588–1679) argued that life in a 'state of nature' (i.e. without leaders and rules) would be 'nasty, brutish and short'. For our own protection, we must have leaders and rules, and this must involve giving up a large amount of personal liberty to enjoy the benefits of living in a stable and ordered society.

Hobbes wrote about a 'social contract' between the rulers and the ruled. In return for the protection of a strong government and the benefits of living in a stable society, we agree to obey the rules.

For Hobbes, this was a justification for what we would now consider to be a dictatorial system of government. Our society has developed considerably, however, as we seek to compromise between the liberty of the individual and the welfare of the wider community.

For **libertarians**, the focus must be firmly on the liberty of the individual, and this is particularly important when it comes to the distribution of money. For a libertarian, justice is being allowed to have what you are entitled to. In the case of personal wealth, you should be allowed to keep your wealth, as long as you acquired it legally. This would mean being in favour of taxes that are as low as possible and government that is as small as possible. Most would agree that there is a need for some taxation, for example to pay for roads, police, prisons and the armed forces. Problems occur when it is suggested that a welfare state should be paid for by taxing the rich.

In the UK, the National Health Service (NHS) is often regarded as offering 'free healthcare'. However, the healthcare is not free; it is in fact extremely expensive. The point of the NHS is that it is 'free at the point of use', i.e. we don't pay when we need to go to a doctor, we pay through taxation. Generally speaking, the richer you are, the more tax you pay. Many rich people opt out of the NHS entirely and pay for private medical care, meaning that they make a large contribution to a health service that they do not actually use.

A libertarian might argue that rich people are being compelled to pay for other people's healthcare and that this is unjust. Rich people are often rich because they have worked hard for their money and they are entitled to keep what they have worked hard for. If everyone were to take out private health insurance and pay for their own healthcare, the result would be lower taxes and more competition between healthcare providers.

The question that arises is how can we care for those members of society who cannot afford to take out private medical insurance? The answer is that these people depend on charity. Human beings have a great capacity for compassion but, for a libertarian, this should be a personal choice. The rich may well choose to help the have-nots, but they should not be obliged to do so. Libertarianism holds that we do not have moral obligations to anyone except ourselves.

Social and economic libertarianism

Libertarianism is not just concerned with money. There are several social issues that interest libertarians.

Libertarians often oppose laws that infringe on personal liberty, especially where there is no obvious victim other than the perpetrator. For example, a libertarian might want to argue against laws restricting prostitution or pornography, as long as there is free consent. If there are willing buyers and willing sellers, they reason that the state should not interfere.

Libertarians have often opposed laws prohibiting the sale of recreational drugs. Certain illegal drugs may be harmful, but the harm is to the person taking these drugs. If that person is a consenting adult, why should the state interfere?

The problem with these views is that there is usually a wider impact, although this is indirect. If a person becomes addicted to heroin, for example, there can be a considerable impact on that person's family and on the wider community.

Should wearing seat belts be compulsory?

It is only relatively recently that the UK government made the wearing of seat belts compulsory. Driving without wearing a seat belt puts you at greater risk of death or serious injury if you are involved in a road traffic accident. Seat belts save lives and the seat-belt laws are credited with significantly cutting the rate of road deaths.

However, some libertarians opposed the laws making seat belts compulsory, not because they thought they were a bad idea but because they regarded it as an infringement of the freedom of the individual to make their use compulsory.

If you choose not to wear a seat belt, who are you potentially hurting, other than yourself?

It is interesting that many economic libertarians happen to be socially conservative. Former British prime minister Margaret Thatcher is often cited as an example.

Egalitarianism

We have seen that libertarians would contend that they are interested in 'justice' and that, for a libertarian, justice is connected with entitlement. People are entitled to what they have, as long as they have acquired their property legally. A major problem is that economic freedom generally leads to serious inequality that can itself be seen as unjust.

Egalitarians are concerned with equality between people. Egalitarian economic theories usually involve a redistribution of wealth by taking from the rich and giving to the poor. This is often done through a system of progressive taxation, in which the rich pay tax at a higher rate, in order to pay for welfare programmes such as unemployment benefit, social housing or a health service that is free at the point of use.

Libertarians argue that a market economy is 'meritocratic', which means that people become rich through their own hard work and talent, and that, therefore, inequality is fair and just because people get what they deserve. The problem is that the world is unfair; people are not always rich because they deserve to be. Is it fair that a million-aire lottery winner is rich just because a particular selection of numbers came up? Is it fair that the market dictates that a Premiership football player can earn £100,000 per week when the player has just been lucky to be born with natural talent? The fact is that some people have more advantages than others, some are blessed with more talent, others are unlucky.

Philosopher John Rawls asked us to imagine what sort of society we would choose to live in, if we had to make a choice 'from behind a veil of ignorance' (*A Theory of Justice*, 1971). Behind the veil of ignorance, we would not know what talents or advantages we would have. We may be healthy or sick, strong or weak, beautiful or ugly, intelligent or unintelligent, talented or untalented. Not knowing these things, Rawls argued, we would choose to live in a fair society with some sort of social safety net to look after those who were unfortunate. Therefore, the rich, the healthy, the strong and the talented have a moral obligation to help those who are less fortunate than themselves through some sort of social welfare system.

Rawls argued that there should be 'equality of opportunity', so that people could compete, as far as possible, on a level playing field. He also argued that society should be arranged, as far as possible, to benefit the least advantaged and the least well off.

One criticism of the veil of ignorance idea is that different people may make different choices. Some people, for example, might be inclined to gamble.

Criticisms of egalitarianism

Economic libertarians have often argued that socialist economies usually fail and that this is disadvantageous to everyone in such societies. Trying to create economic equality by removing too much of the wealth of the rich reduces the incentive to work. A story by American comedian Bob Newhart illustrates this principle. In his early working life, he claimed to have been employed as a clerk in his local unemployment office, earning $60 a week, but he quit when he learned that the claimants were receiving $55 a week, '...and they only had to come in one day a week to collect it!'

For many people, money is a powerful incentive to work harder. In a similar way, profit is a powerful incentive for businesses. Where there is competition between privately owned businesses, there is an incentive to improve the quality of the product, to innovate, to keep prices competitive and to retain the loyalty of the customer.

Another important economic factor is the 'trickle-down effect'. It has often been argued that people who work hard and create wealth for themselves also create wealth for others. If a capitalist, through hard work, talent and willingness to risk everything, creates a large and successful business, others will benefit from that business through increased employment opportunities. Some have argued that if rich people are taxed at a lower rate, they will create more wealth through investment that leads to economic growth than if they were taxed heavily to fund welfare programmes.

The major difference between the libertarian and the egalitarian approach seems to be over the question of whether or not we have a moral obligation to those less well off than ourselves. Libertarianism, in its most extreme form, takes the view that charity is entirely optional; whereas the egalitarian approach is that we do have a moral responsibility to others. For a libertarian, justice is based on entitlement, with people being entitled to keep what they acquire legally, but egalitarians believe that people have 'rights', which create obligations in others.

Rights and responsibilities

Both libertarians and egalitarians would agree that human beings have rights that can be seen as entitlements, which create obligations (responsibilities) in others. There is disagreement about what rights are, where they come from and how useful they are as principles.

If we live in a society that is based on some sort of social contract, we can see that agreements exist in which, for example, people agree not to harm each other. A law may be established in which theft becomes illegal. Because people have a right to property, we must also accept the obligation to refrain from stealing the property of others. Murder and assault are illegal, so we have the obligation to refrain from violently attacking other people. It is important to note that each right is accompanied by an obligation to others.

Libertarians value the right to property and also freedom of choice, i.e. freedom to live your life as you wish as long as there is no significant infringement of the freedom of others. Believing that we have moral obligations towards the less well off, egalitarians are more likely to emphasise social and economic rights, such as the right to a minimum wage and the right to universal healthcare. Egalitarians may also emphasise the importance of the right to equal treatment without discrimination on grounds of gender, race or age.

Sometimes there is a codified 'bill of rights' that is part of the basic law of a country. In the USA, for example, citizens have a right to bear arms, which limits the power of the state to take their guns away. In the UK, there is a system whereby people traditionally have the right to do anything, if there is no law against it. For example, certain drugs are banned; if a drug is not banned, it follows that people have the right to use it.

Civil rights are often contrasted with human rights, which are said to apply to all human beings irrespective of the society in which they live. Civil rights apply only to the citizens of one country. For example, in the UK, an attempt to limit freedom of speech may be regarded as a breach of civil rights, yet in other countries, in which there is no tradition of freedom of speech, such civil rights could not be asserted. Nevertheless, violations of freedom of speech in any country could be said to violate human rights.

The idea of human rights arises from theories of 'natural rights' that exist whether or not society chooses to uphold them. Those most commonly suggested are the rights to life, liberty and property. The US Constitution, for example, asserts that it is 'self evident' that a right to 'life, liberty and the pursuit of happiness' exists. The idea of natural rights is that human beings will follow their nature and that it is wrong for governments to try to stop them; many have tried, however, and this limits the usefulness of the concept of natural rights.

After all, what is the point of having a right that cannot be enforced? Utilitarian philosopher Jeremy Bentham (1748–1832) described the idea of natural rights as 'nonsense upon stilts', and many others have taken the view that rights exist only if they create responsibilities in others.

However, international organisations such as the United Nations have asserted that human rights can be said to be important, whether or not a particular country chooses to respect them. In a repressive dictatorship, there may be a serious lack of basic civil liberties such as the right to free speech or the right to a fair trial. The international community may seek to put pressure on such a country to respect basic human rights that it sees as universal. If we believe in universal human rights, we are asserting that there are some entitlements that must transcend national boundaries or cultural customs.

Problems with human rights

It is easy to claim rights but less easy to accept the obligations they entail. If medical care is a human right, someone has to pay for it. If 'poverty' is a violation of human rights, it follows that the richer members of society must be taxed in order to improve the standard of living of the less well off until everyone is raised above whatever is set as the poverty threshold.

Human rights can clash with the desire for national security and the need to prevent crime. For example, the risk of terrorism has led some to advocate the detention without trial and even the torture of terrorist suspects. The problem of crime has led to a large increase in the use of CCTV, which could be said to infringe the right to privacy. Freedom can be seen as a negative or a positive thing: we can have the freedom *to* do something or we can demand the freedom *from* something. For example, the right to privacy may dictate that we should have the freedom to walk down the street without having our movements filmed, whereas others may assert that it is more important to protect the right to be free from crime. CCTV is often welcomed by a majority of people, who believe it can deter and detect crime, despite the loss of personal privacy.

Rights: examination tip

Rights can be used as principles in the F503 examination, but it is important to consider exactly what right is being claimed and whether or not it *can be* claimed. Is it a civil right or a human right? Can it be asserted as a universal right? Can it be enforced? What obligations does it create in others?

Do you have the right to an opinion?

People often claim that they have the 'right to an opinion', but what exactly do they mean? What sort of right is being claimed and what obligations does it create in others?

Presumably people are asserting a civil right to free speech. Such a right is certainly not universally held. Even in the UK, there are some limits, such as restrictions on racist speech or incitement.

If we do have a right to express an opinion, others do not have an obligation to agree with our opinions or even to listen to what we have to say. The right to an opinion is simply the right to hold an opinion and possibly to be allowed to express that opinion without there being any guarantee that anyone will listen.

Exercise: Do you have the right?

The following are rights that are sometimes claimed. For each of these rights, consider whether it is a human or a civil right, how the right can be enforced and what obligations are created in others.

- the right to life
- the right to clean water
- the right to privacy
- the right to choose
- the right to protest

Case study: The erosion of British liberties

In the summer of 2008, leading Conservative politician David Davis resigned his parliamentary seat to force a by-election. His protest was against the government's decision to pass a law allowing the detention of terrorist suspects, without trial, for 42 days. He objected to this measure as it was the latest in a series of powers taken by the state that could be used against innocent people.

Opposing him was Jill Saward, who argued that the police should be allowed to use such measures in order to protect the public from crime. Saward was 21 years old when she was raped in her father's vicarage in Ealing by a violent gang, who also beat her boyfriend and her father.

Both candidates claimed to be in favour of 'freedom' but differed about what it meant. Writing in the *Independent* ('What sort of freedom do you believe in?', 9 July 2008), commentator Johann Hari observed that:

> Like opposing Robert Mugabe and cuddling puppies, everybody in Britain is theoretically in favour of freedom. But the battle in Haltemprice and Howden [Davis's parliamentary constituency] is a slap-in-the-face reminder that we fundamentally disagree about what freedom means — so we are increasingly shouting at each other across a chasm of miscomprehension.

Davis and Saward saw 'freedom' very differently. Davis was arguing that, to be free, the citizen needs to be protected from the power of the state. Saward argued that giving the state power can protect citizens from each other.

In addition to opposing 42-day detention, Davis argued against the use of the national DNA database, which is the biggest of its kind in the world. It holds the DNA of millions of citizens, many of whom have not committed any offence. He also objected to CCTV, pointing out that there is one CCTV camera for every 14 British citizens and yet the technology is used to solve only 3% of crimes. Together with the proposed ID cards, he claimed that such powers represented 'an erosion of British liberties'.

Saward's argument was that the police should be allowed to use these powers fully to catch criminals who are a threat to the liberty of others. Although it is relatively new, Saward pointed out that the DNA database had already helped to catch 114 murderers and 184 sex offenders. She claimed to be upholding the freedom of the potential victims who could be spared. She did not see that the liberty of the individual was threatened by people being filmed by CCTV because only those with something to hide should be concerned about its use.

Hari quoted Isaiah Berlin, who said, 'Liberty is the absence of obstacles to the fulfilment of your desires'. The state can put obstacles in your way but it can also clear obstacles, such as terrorism, murder and rape, from your path.

Animal rights

Traditionally, ethical theories relate to human beings: how we should behave and how we ought to treat each other. In Western traditions, it is only relatively recently that some have questioned whether or not our 'circle of moral concern' should be expanded to include other members of the animal kingdom.

The traditional view is summed up by Aristotle, who believed that animals have no moral status because, unlike us, they are devoid of reason. He considered that animals exist only for the benefit of human beings. This can be described as an **anthropocentric** (human-centred) view.

Believing that animals are devoid of reason, human beings have traditionally caged, killed, eaten and experimented on other species. Can this exploitation be justified simply because humans, unlike other species, are rational creatures?

One problem is that not all humans are rational. Babies are not capable of reason, nor are those who are severely mentally ill, yet we regard such people as worthy of equal rights with other humans.

A further justification for an anthropocentric approach is that human beings can understand reality only from a human point of view. We are not capable of understanding how a cat or a flea sees the universe. Therefore, what makes us happy is not necessarily what makes other species happy.

Nevertheless, we can see that other species are capable of suffering, and this has led some people to adopt a position of 'animal welfare', in which we try to avoid causing unnecessary pain and suffering to other animals, not least because needlessly doing so could be said to diminish us as humans.

Australian philosopher Peter Singer goes much further than minimising unnecessary suffering. In his book *Animal Liberation* (1975), he argues that, in deciding whether or not animals can be said to have rights, we should focus not on the capacity to reason but on the capacity to feel pain and suffer.

According to Singer, human beings give a disproportionate amount of moral weight to our own species, generally disregarding the pain and suffering of other animals. This approach can be called 'speciesism', which is discriminating against another species. Some might regard speciesism as analogous to racism or sexism.

Criticisms of animal rights

Critics of the concept of animal rights argue that animals do not have the capacity to enter into a social contract or to make moral choices. They cannot respect the rights of others or even understand the concept of rights. Morality is a human invention and only human beings can make moral decisions, at least as far as we understand them. The weakness of this criticism is that it seems to return to the view that only humans have rights because only humans are rational. Babies and people with very severe learning disabilities do not make moral decisions, yet they are still said to have moral rights.

Environmental ethics

It is a struggle to persuade some people that all humans are entitled to moral consideration, and only a minority would agree that other species of animals have moral rights. So what hope is there that philosophers might be able to persuade us that plants or rocks should be part of our moral decision making?

From an anthropocentric point of view, the world exists for humans to use or exploit for our own benefit. However, in other cultures, there is a strong belief that human beings cannot *own* the land. In 1854, a Native American chief was presented with an offer to buy tribal lands. Part of his response, the famous Testimony of Chief Seattle, was:

> How can you buy or sell the sky, the warmth of the land? The idea is strange to us. If we do not own the freshness of the air and the sparkle of the water, how can you buy them?
>
> Every part of this Earth is sacred to my people. Every shining pine needle, every sandy shore, every mist in the dark woods, every clearing and humming insect is holy in the memory and experience of my people. The sap which courses through the trees carries the memory of the red man.

Similar sentiments were expressed by Crocodile Dundee when he was asked what he thought of land rights for Australian aborigines. His response was that people arguing over who owns the land was 'like two fleas arguing over who owns the dog'.

Nevertheless, human beings have exploited the natural resources of the planet and now face an environmental crisis. Environmental ethics asserts that human beings should 'widen the circle of moral concern' to include not only other animals but potentially everything else that shares this planet. There is apparently an urgent need to take greater care of the planet, but how can this be expressed as an ethical principle?

Ecological ethics

The ecological view is that we should concentrate not on individual rights but on the overall importance of diversity and the interrelatedness of all things on the planet. For their survival, humans depend on things that are not human, and the same can be said of every other species. We should think less about the value of individuals and consider much more our value as part of a collective.

In response, Peter Singer, who wants to expand the circle of moral worth to other species of animal, rejects the idea of extending moral consideration to plants, gases and rocks. His reasoning is that animals are important because they are 'sentient', whereas other things are not. Plants and rocks are not capable of suffering and we have no way of knowing what interests they might have.

Conservation ethics

A more popular approach is to acknowledge that, although rocks, gases and plants do not have any intrinsic value, they are important for human beings. Human beings must protect the environment simply because it is in our interests to do so. This could be seen as an anthropocentric view because it affirms the idea that the resources of the planet exist for the benefit of human beings; but it emphasises the importance of looking after the planet much better than we previously have done, because we will suffer if we do not.

If human beings need to consider the environment in their moral decision making, some adjustments might need to be made to traditional ethical theories. Environmental issues have caused some problems for libertarians, who would traditionally argue that the government should not intervene to restrict the activities of businesses that might cause environmental damage in the pursuit of greater profits. Recently, some 'geolibertarians' have argued that certain natural resources, such as land, should not be considered as personal property, which would seem to echo the sentiments of Chief Seattle.

Human beings are also being asked to consider the moral interests not only of people who are alive today but also of future generations. For example, a utilitarian happiness calculation would traditionally involve weighing up the happiness of people who are around at the time. However, the effects of environmentally damaging activities may be felt many years from now, so utilitarians should perhaps also take account of the interests of those who are yet to be born.

Case study: Are climate change deniers like Josef Fritzl?

When the crimes of Josef Fritzl emerged in April 2008, the case shocked the world. Fritzl had imprisoned his daughter in an underground cellar for 24 years, repeatedly raped her and fathered her seven children.

In June 2008, the Bishop of Stafford, Gordon Mursell, caused a storm of controversy when, in a parish letter, he appeared to claim that people who refused to respond appropriately to the crisis of global warming were 'as guilty as' Josef Fritzl. His argument drew a furious response from various columnists, including Ruth Gledhill of *The Times*.

The Bishop's analogy

The Bishop's argument was that natural disasters, such as the 2004 tsunami in the Indian Ocean and Cyclone Nagis in Myanmar (Burma) in 2008, have caused great human suffering. If we could have done something to save lives, would we have done it? If it is true that disasters such as these are caused by global warming, the answer is possibly not, because many people deny that climate change is caused by human activity and refuse to change their environmentally damaging lifestyles.

According to the Bishop, such people could be said to be like Josef Fritzl for two reasons. First, they are 'in effect locking our children and grandchildren into a world with no future and throwing away the key'. They are also behaving self-ishly in putting their own desires before those of other people or of future gen-erations. Like Josef Fritzl, they subscribe to the philosophy that 'I will do what makes me happy and if that causes others to suffer, hard luck'.

Extract from Ruth Gledhill's response

In his statement, the Bishop insisted that he was 'simply trying to use an anal-ogy to get people to wake up to the consequences of what we are failing to do'. He insisted that he was not saying that people who refuse to accept the reality of climate change are child abusers. Gledhill's response was:

> I have to interject here or I'll explode. Dear, dear silly bishop, you are being reported as having said this because it is what you said... As Homer Simpson says, 'D'oh!!!'

> For myself, I am proud to put my family first. Yes, I put feeding my family before feeding the thousands made homeless in China... That's why we are all so furious.

Source: the statement from the Bishop of Stafford and Gledhill's response are from Gledhill's blog on *Times Online* (2 June 2008) www.timesonline.co.uk.

The Bishop's analogy may have been clumsy and tasteless, and he eventually apolo-gised for that, but he did not apologise for raising the issue. His analogy was part of a clear argument in favour of environmental ethics and an altruistic approach.

Perhaps the weakest part of the Bishop's argument is in his use of examples — of the tsunami and the cyclone. He uses hypothetical reasoning in raising the question of whether we *would* have acted *if* we *could* have done something to save lives but then he seems to proceed on the assumption that the disasters *were* caused by climate change, that the climate change *was* caused by human activity and that there is, there-fore, a direct causal link between the behaviour of climate change deniers and the natural disasters in Asia.

The reliability of these assumptions is highly questionable. Natural disasters happen even without climate change, and although environmentalists claim that climate change increases their frequency and severity, it is impossible to know that we could have prevented specific incidents. A significant minority dispute the claims that global warming is caused by human activity, and others believe that, although human activity probably *is* responsible for the warming, anything that we now do to try to slow it down or reverse it may not have any effect for a long time, as greenhouse gases have such a long atmospheric lifetime.

If 'climate change deniers' are unwilling to accept the reality of global warming, it is difficult to see how they can be accused of acting selfishly. Perhaps a better target for the analogy would have been those who do accept that global warming can be slowed down or reversed by people adopting green lifestyles, yet who refuse to do so themselves.

The weakness in Gledhill's response is that she apparently failed to understand the Bishop's use of an analogy in his argument. Despite her reference to Homer Simpson, the Bishop did **not** say that climate change deniers *are* child abusers. The point of his analogy was that they are *like* child abusers in two specific respects, which he explained.

In the first respect, the analogy could be said to be strong because failing to prevent global warming does not have a direct or immediate impact. Instead, its effects will be felt by future generations, who will have to live with the consequences of our current lifestyles. This is why environmental ethics urges human beings to include future generations, including children yet unborn, in our circle of moral worth.

Failing to consider the interests of these future generations is a selfish act because we are putting our pleasure before that of others. Gledhill seems to be asserting a false choice between feeding her family and feeding the refugees in China. In so doing, she has not addressed the Bishop's argument that we should alter our lifestyles to minimise environmentally damaging activities.

Learning and Careers

Questions
&
Answers

This section contains a sample Unit F503 paper and resource booklet. Read the documents carefully and answer the questions that follow.

In this section, model A-grade answers, as well as C-grade responses, are provided for each question. Answers are accompanied by an examiner's commentary (indicated by the symbol 🄴), with an explanation of the shortcomings of the poorer responses and an outline of how these answers could be improved.

Examiner's advice on how to tackle questions 3 and 4 is provided before the sample answers to these questions. This is also indicated by the symbol 🄴.

Resource booklet

Document 1: Alternate weekly collection systems

In the UK, 144 local councils have switched to alternate weekly collection (AWC) systems of bin collection, whereby household rubbish is collected one week and recyclable waste the next. The Local Government Association (LGA) claims that these councils recycle or compost 30% of what they collect, compared to only 23% among the authorities that are not using these systems. The LGA says that the top ten councils for recycling all use AWC systems. It estimates that, if AWC were used across the whole country, it could cut landfill use by 1.2m tonnes and save £22m in landfill fees.

The LGA claims that most people questioned say that they have no problem with AWC systems but they might be unsuitable in cities like London where many people live in flats. Some Conservative MPs, however, claim that allowing councils to offer households financial incentives for recycling might amount to a stealth tax with people having to pay again for collections that have already been paid for through council tax. Others are concerned that there could be an increase in fly tipping (illegal dumping of waste) if people were to be charged to have their rubbish collected.

Others are concerned about health risks, especially if food waste is not collected every week. World Health Organization (WHO) guidelines are that rubbish should be collected every week, and a Canadian study suggested that asthma rates increased when rubbish was collected less frequently. Other reports indicate that flies, smells and rodent populations could increase. A spokesperson for the Department for Environment, Food and Rural Affairs (DEFRA) has called for 'proper education about what to do with waste food'.

The latest proposal is a 'pay as you throw' scheme, in which wheelie bins would be fitted with microchips that would be read as they are emptied by the refuse vehicle. Households would then be sent a bill for the amount of waste that they throw out.

The aim is to reduce the amount of rubbish sent to landfill sites. Landfill sites waste resources and chew up land. It is estimated that England will run out of landfill space in nine years. Methane from landfill accounts for 3% of the UK's climate change emissions. Britain recycles only 27% of its household rubbish, compared to 65% in the Netherlands.

Document 2: The Daily Mail's 'Campaign to Save Weekly Rubbish Collections'

Of the 216 councils that still pick up the bins once a week, 21 managed recycling levels higher than the 30% average among those that have downgraded their service. Two, Cotswold in Gloucestershire and Three Rivers in Hertfordshire, are listed by the LGA among the ten councils with the most improved recycling rates in the country. At the bottom of the LGA lists are a number of councils that have brought in compulsory recycling and fortnightly collections, yet have failed in their aim of recycling any large proportion of their waste.

Critics say that nine years is plenty of time to find new landfill, and there is plenty of suitable space in Britain. EU legislation against landfill was brought in largely at the request of countries such as Holland, which have genuine difficulties finding room.

Many other countries achieve higher recycling rates than Britain, while still offering daily or twice-weekly refuse collections. For example:

- The USA has rubbish collections two to three times per week and has a recycling rate of 32%. Recycling is not compulsory, but is promoted through publicity campaigns.
- In France, rubbish collection is daily for city apartments and at least weekly elsewhere. The recycling rate is 30%.
- In Spain, rubbish collection is daily in cities and two to three times a week elsewhere. The country has a recycling rate of 35%.
- Switzerland has rubbish collections once to twice per week and a recycling rate of 51%. There are strong financial incentives because recycling is free but rubbish collections are not.
- Germany, like the UK, has fortnightly rubbish collections in some areas and weekly collections in others. The recycling rate is 57%. There are strict rules and fines of up to £600 for failing to recycle.

Source: adapted from an article by Steve Doughty, the *Daily Mail* (24 April 2007)

Document 3: House of Commons and local government committee report on refuse collection

AWC [alternate weekly collection] schemes have frequently been characterised by 'fortnightly'; in fact, in all cases, refuse is collected weekly, just not all refuse every week. Councillor Paul Bettison offered a simple alternative, used by his Bracknell Forest District Council, of 'alternate bin collection', adding that this let them use the slogan 'It's as easy as ABC!'

Gary Alderson, Director of Environmental and Planning Services for Mid-Beds Council, told the House of Commons Committee that his council saved £700,000 in its first year of AWC, partly because splitting collection vehicles to collect both residual and recyclable wastes allowed it to reduce the number of vehicles needed.

The Minister for Waste told the committee that 19 of the 20 English authorities with the best recycling rates had adapted AWC schemes. The principle underlying these recycling increases is that AWC makes householders sort their waste into recyclable and residual waste, because the capacity to dispose of residual waste is limited.

The most widespread criticism of AWC has focused on the disposal of food waste, largely on arguments that non-collection for up to 14 days could result in health risks from increased fly and maggot populations, from bags being torn by birds or foxes, and from unpleasant smells. The government believes there are 'strong arguments for encouraging more separate collection of food waste'.

Around one third of all food bought in the UK is not eaten but disposed of, says WRAP [Waste & Resources Action Programme]. Reasons may include poor house-hold meal planning and over-purchase of foodstuffs, including those with soon-to-pass sell-by dates and perishable goods, such as fruit, on two-for-one or half-price offers. An average household throws away £400 worth of food per year.

DEFRA denies that AWC increases health risks. Gary Alderson, Director of Environmental and Planning Services for Mid-Beds Council, said: 'We have had [AWC] in 54,000 houses over two years now and we have not seen epidemics and new diseases coming.'

Source: extracts from the House of Commons and Local Government Committee Report on
Refuse Collection (10 July 2007)

Document 4: Landfill waste

The UK was labelled 'the dustbin of Europe' after the Local Government Association reported that Britain was dumping more household waste into landfill sites than any other country in the European Union. However, the UK does better than Bulgaria and Ireland when the amount per person is calculated.

There were 22.6 million tonnes of rubbish sent to landfill in the UK in 2004/05. Although this figure has fallen since 2005, other European countries have also cut their landfill use.

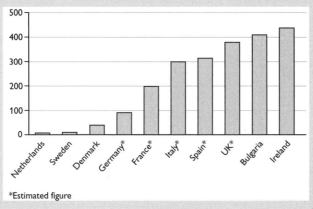

Landfill waste in EU countries in 2005 (kg/person)

*Estimated figure

Source: Eurostat

Sample examination paper

Read the documents in the resource booklet (pages 47–49) and answer the questions that follow.

1   Identify and explain *two* problems that might arise in using Documents 1 and 4 to assess the extent to which the UK can be regarded as the 'dustbin of Europe'.   (4 marks)

2   Refer to Document 3. Explain why the term 'alternate weekly collection' might present problems of definition.   (4 marks)

3   There are a number of choices that we could make about rubbish collection systems. These choices may be influenced by a number of criteria (such as public opinion). Evaluate one such choice by reference to appropriate criteria and to the documents in the resource booklet.   (20 marks)

4   (a) State and explain one dilemma that arises in making decisions about refuse collection systems.   (2 marks)

    (b) Write an argument that attempts to resolve the dilemma you have identified. In your argument you should identify and use relevant principles (these may be derived from ethical theories), supporting your answer with material from the resource booklet.   (30 marks)

Paper total: 60 marks

Sample answers

Problems arising from the documents

Identify and explain *two* problems that might arise in using Documents 1 and 4 to assess the extent to which the UK can be regarded as the 'dustbin of Europe'.   (4 marks)

■ ■ ■

A-grade answer

Is the UK really the 'dustbin of Europe'? Document 1 says that Britain recycles 27% of its waste, compared to 65% in Holland. This seems to be a significant difference, but the example of Holland has apparently been chosen because it is at the top of the European recycling league. Every country looks bad when compared to the Dutch.

In Document 4, we can see which countries send the most waste to landfill. The UK sent the most, but this is partly because the UK has a much higher population than most European countries. A more relevant statistic is the *per capita* figure, which is shown in the chart. When the landfill waste is shown in terms of kilograms per person, the UK manages to do better than Ireland and Bulgaria, although we still seem to be doing badly.

📝 It is important not to spend too much time on the introductory questions. As you can see, the higher marks are allocated to the later questions.

This sample answer is appropriately concise. It is focused on two problems and it clearly addresses the issue of whether or not the UK is the 'dustbin of Europe'.

A further issue that could be explored is that Document 1 asserts that 'England will run out of landfill space in nine years'. It would appear that the assertion is based on an assumption that no new landfill sites will open and this is somewhat misleading, although there is considerable potential for opposition to new landfill sites on grounds of pollution and the impact on wildlife.

■ ■ ■

C-grade answer

Document 1 says that Britain recycles 27% of its waste, compared to 65% in Holland but Britain is a much bigger country than Holland, so there is bound to be more waste.

The countries that send less waste to landfill are not necessarily recycling more. They may be dumping rubbish at sea or dumping it in other countries.

The first point illustrates a common confusion about percentages and why they are used instead of actual amounts. Because the amount has been expressed as a percentage, the problem of Britain having a larger population has been removed. The figures do take the different populations into account.

The second point does raise a relevant issue, which is that there is not necessarily a simple choice between sending rubbish to landfill and recycling. The assertion that 'we must increase recycling in order to reduce landfill' is a false choice, since there are alternatives. Some countries could be achieving low rates of landfill by incinerating a great deal of their waste.

Question 2

Problems of definition

Refer to Document 3. Explain why the term 'alternate weekly collection' might present problems of definition. (4 marks)

■ ■ ■

A-grade answer

It is clear that the name given to the system is seen as important. Opponents of the new refuse collection systems often refer to 'fortnightly rubbish collection' because general waste is collected fortnightly. It was previously collected weekly and this represents a decline in the service being provided by their local councils.

Supporters of the new systems usually insist on calling the new system AWC (alternate weekly collection) and they would insist that it is misleading to say that rubbish collection is fortnightly because there is still a collection every week, just not all waste every week.

So, both names would seem to be technically correct but also somewhat misleading. Councillor Paul Bettison's suggestion is to call the system ABC (alternate bin collection) and he suggests the slogan 'It's as easy as ABC!' This could be a useful suggestion, since it clarifies the system of alternating bins rather than weeks.

🖉 This answer is appropriately concise. It accurately identifies the problem of definition arising from the terminology.

■ ■ ■

C-grade answer

AWC is the correct term because your rubbish is collected every week. They alternate between collecting the black bin one week and the green bin the next, so it is not true to say that they are only collecting fortnightly.

🖉 This candidate has understood why the supporters of AWC systems have argued that the term 'fortnightly rubbish collection' is misleading.

The candidate's answer would be improved by including an explicit reference to the document.

The major weakness in this response is that the candidate seems to understand only one side of the argument. Supporters of AWC are keen to avoid the use of the word 'fortnightly' because it draws attention to the decline in the level of service that has taken place. Opponents of the new rubbish collection systems are keen to use the word 'fortnightly' because they want to emphasise that general waste is now collected only every fortnight.

Question **3**

Choices and criteria

There are a number of choices that we could make about rubbish collection systems. These choices may be influenced by a number of criteria (such as public opinion). Evaluate one such choice by reference to appropriate criteria and to the documents in the resource booklet. (20 marks)

■ ■ ■

Having read the resource booklet and thought about the issue, you should think about the range of choices that might be available and the criteria that can be used to make choices.

You might identify the following as choices:
- increase collections to twice a week or daily in some areas (e.g. for apartment blocks)
- retain weekly rubbish collection
- pursue AWC with exceptions (e.g. special collections for food waste or exceptions for apartment blocks)
- provide AWC for all
- provide AWC with punitive fines for failing to recycle
- introduction of 'pay as you throw' schemes

You might identify the following as criteria:
- cost
- public health
- legal considerations
- practicability
- human rights
- animal welfare
- public opinion
- environmental concerns
- effectiveness

In tackling this question, you must apply several criteria to one of the choices and evaluate the *relevance* of these criteria in order to argue a case. In this context, the word 'relevance' can be taken to mean 'usefulness' or 'importance'. You could argue that a given criterion is or is not relevant to the choice.

You are also expected to make critical comments about material in the resource booklet to inform your answers.

■ ■ ■

A-grade answer

In this answer, the candidate seeks to apply three criteria to the choice of introducing AWC systems for all.

Criterion of environmental concerns

In Document 1, the Local Government Association (LGA) reports that the 144 councils that use the alternate weekly collection system have a better recycling rate than those that do not. The difference is 7%. This would suggest that alternate weekly collection does increase recycling rates.

This conclusion is challenged by the *Daily Mail* in Document 2. It observes that there are some councils using AWC systems with poor recycling rates but other councils with weekly collections have high recycling rates. These councils are exceptions to a general rule, but they do demonstrate that an AWC system is neither a necessary nor a sufficient condition of having a good record for recycling.

If there is a general correlation between AWC collection systems and comparatively high recycling rates, it is tempting to conclude, as the LGA has, that the AWC system has in some way caused the recycling. To do so, however, would be to risk confusing correlation with causation because further investigation is needed.

First, in the case of the councils with AWC systems, did the recycling rates increase after the AWC system was introduced, or could it be the case that these areas had high recycling rates even before AWC?

Second, even if the recycling rates did improve after the introduction of AWC, it cannot automatically be concluded that it was the AWC scheme that *caused* the increase in recycling. It may have been, for example, that the introduction of the AWC scheme was accompanied by a pro-recycling publicity campaign or an improvement in local recycling facilities.

Criterion of cost

Cost is clearly an important issue for local councils in making choices about their refuse collection systems. Any system where the householder has to do more and the binman has to do less is likely to be beneficial for the council in terms of cost. In Document 3, Gary Alderson told the House of Commons Committee that his council saved £700,000 in its first year of AWC, partly because splitting collection vehicles to collect both residual and recyclable wastes allowed it to reduce the number of vehicles needed. However, an even bigger cost motivation for local councils is likely to be the threat of penalty charges for exceeding landfill quotas.

Document 1 claims that the taxpayer could save '£22m in landfill fees' if AWC was to be implemented nationwide, although it cannot automatically be concluded that the cost savings would result in reductions in council tax, since the councils could use the money for other purposes. It does seem likely, however, that the UK will face EU fines, unless it cuts the amount of rubbish sent to landfill, and that taxpayers are likely to pick up the bill. Although members of the public are likely to be attracted by the prospect of a convenient rubbish collection system, they might be reluctant to pay higher taxes.

Criterion of public health

Public health is an issue that has been raised by the opponents of AWC, with the reasoning that flies, maggots and rats could be attracted to rubbish, especially food

waste, that is left uncollected for a fortnight. In Document 3, Gary Alderson said: 'We have had [AWC] in 54,000 houses over two years now and we have not seen epidemics and new diseases coming.' Alderson's comments would not seem to be particularly reassuring. Just because there have been no new diseases or epidemics in his area in a 2-year period, it cannot automatically be concluded that the new collection systems do not pose a risk to public health.

The DEFRA spokesperson in Document 1 suggests that there should be 'proper education about what to do with waste food'. It may be true that properly wrapped waste food can be left for a fortnight without posing a risk to health but, even with a public education campaign, some people will be more careful than others. This could be a particular problem for people living in blocks of flats where there are communal bins, especially during the summer months. Therefore, there could be a strong case for collecting food waste at least weekly, especially for certain types of housing and at certain times of the year.

> This candidate has clearly divided up the answer with three headings to show that three different criteria are being applied to one choice.
>
> There are frequent and critical references to the material in the documents.
>
> There are some strong evaluative comments about the relevance and importance of the criteria with reference to the choice of AWC systems.

■ ■ ■

C-grade answers

> The following are extracts from answers of various candidates, applying different criteria to different choices.

Choice: 'pay as you throw'

Criterion: practicability

If a system of 'pay as you throw' were introduced, this would be highly impractical. This is because if every household's waste has to be weighed, then this would make rubbish collections take longer, as having to weigh every bin adds to the workload of the council workers.

> This is a short answer but it does identify, briefly, one reason why the 'pay as you throw' solution may be impractical. However, there are no references to the documents in the resource booklet. Closer examination of Document 1 would reveal that it is not the council workers who are weighing the bins, but rather the collection trucks that read microchips on the bins to calculate the usage of each household. Whether this is a practical solution would depend on whether this technology would work in practice. If it would not, it would clearly cause many problems since households may get inaccurate bills.

Choice: AWC for all

Criterion: legal considerations

If AWC were introduced for all, then people may begin to sue councils if for instance rat infestations become common. This is because they would raise problems for residents and people could then blame the council for not collecting the rubbish. Document 1 says that flies and rat problems could become more common because rubbish would not be collected as frequently.

> 🖉 There is a reference to the resource booklet in this answer but it is selective. The claim that rat populations may increase needs to be considered critically. For example, the candidate could refer to the response of the DEFRA spokesman calling for 'proper education about what to do with waste food'. If people dispose of waste food properly, then rat infestations may not be a problem after all. If they do not dispose of food waste properly, then the courts may decide that it is the householders rather than the council who are responsible for the infestations.

Choice: more frequent collections

Criterion: practicability

If it is decided that everyone should be given more frequent rubbish collections then the question of practicability must be raised. It is likely that it will not be practical to collect everyone's rubbish more often, with the current available resources. Furthermore, it is believed that more frequent rubbish collections will produce more rubbish and it may not be practical to store this.

> 🖉 This candidate needs to refer to the documents in the resource booklet and to be more critical with this material. The candidate is right that there are claims that AWC can reduce the amount of rubbish produced, by increasing recycling rates, but there are also counterclaims, such as those in Document 2.
>
> This candidate has also confused cost with practicability. Councils *could* collect rubbish more frequently if they wanted to, but this would increase the cost of the rubbish collection system, which could in turn lead to increased council tax.

Choice: AWC for all

Criterion: human rights

AWC for all will lead to issues with human rights. Local authorities claim AWC collections are weekly, however essentially they take place every two weeks. Consequently, rubbish may begin to rot and degrade, resulting in a bad smell and in worst case scenarios rat infestations. This problem is even more pronounced in tower blocks and apartments. In these establishments, large numbers of people share the same bin. As a result, these bins are large in size and contain large amounts of rubbish. Therefore the associated problems are exaggerated and may potentially pose a health risk. AWC therefore may conflict with people's human rights.

 The problem with this answer is that the candidate does not explain why human rights are a relevant criterion to use in this case. What are these human rights that councils could be violating? Do people really have a right to be healthy and is it the obligation of the local council to ensure that people's bins do not attract rats? In this case, it would probably be easier to argue that human rights is not a relevant criterion.

Resolving dilemmas

(a) **State and explain one dilemma that arises in making decisions about refuse collection systems.** (2 marks)

■ ■ ■

Candidate A

What sort of rubbish collection service should councils provide?

Candidate B

Should councils provide weekly collection of all rubbish or should they introduce AWC systems to encourage recycling?

Candidate C

Should councils introduce AWC rubbish collection systems, even though there could be unpopularity, smell, inconvenience and dangers to public health, or should they retain weekly collection of all rubbish and risk having to pay penalty charges for exceeding their landfill quotas?

Candidate A would be unlikely to get any marks at all. This candidate asks a vague question and there is no clear choice or explanation of the problem.

Candidate B does offer a clear choice, but there is no explanation of the problems arising from each choice. This would be a C-grade response.

Candidate C deserves both marks because there is a clear choice and a good explanation of the dilemma. This candidate shows that there are problems arising from either choice. Note that, with only 2 marks available, there is no need to write more than one sentence. This would be an A-grade response.

■ ■ ■

(b) **Write an argument that attempts to resolve the dilemma you have identified. In your argument you should identify and use relevant principles (these may be derived from ethical theories), supporting your answer with material from the resource booklet.** (30 marks)

For part (b) you would be expected to choose three or four relevant principles to resolve the dilemma.

Explain the principles briefly. Simply stating 'utilitarianism', for example, would be inadequate because this is the name of an ethical theory, rather than a statement of a principle. 'The utilitarian principle that we should act in a way that would result in the greatest happiness for the greatest number' would be a sufficiently clear statement of a principle.

question

You then need to apply the principles to the dilemma. For example, in the case of the utilitarian principle, this would mean performing a happiness calculation and explaining what decision the principle would seem to support.

Now you need to judge the effectiveness of the principles. None of the principles explained in this guide is without its critics and you need to show that you are aware of the major criticisms.

As with the previous questions, you are expected to make critical judgements about the usefulness of the evidence in the resource booklet. You could repeat comments made in your answers to the earlier questions where these are relevant to the argument being developed.

You should aim to develop an effective argument containing the following elements:
- clear strands of reasoning
- intermediate conclusions
- hypothetical reasoning
- anticipation of and effective response to counter-arguments
- a clearly stated conclusion

You should be familiar with these elements from Unit F502. You need to avoid flaws, inconsistency and unreasonable assumptions.

■ ■ ■

A-grade answer

Dilemma to be resolved:

'Should councils introduce AWC rubbish collection systems, even though there could be unpopularity, smell, inconvenience and dangers to public health, or should they retain weekly collection of all rubbish and risk having to pay penalty charges for exceeding their landfill quotas?'

This argument will consider the policy of many local councils to introduce alternate weekly collection of refuse. The AWC system is often called 'fortnightly rubbish collection', but this is misleading since there is always a weekly collection but not of *all* refuse. Under an AWC system, general refuse and recyclable refuse is collected on alternate weeks.

The democratic principle could be used to resolve this dilemma. In a democratic system something should be done if the majority wants it, and it is clear that AWC systems have been unpopular in some quarters. In Document 1, the Local Government Association claims that a majority of people have no problems with the new system but that is not the same thing as saying that the majority of people support the new system. Document 1 also shows that many MPs are opposed to the AWC system, and Document 2 shows that a national newspaper is campaigning against it.

Public opinion, however, can be fickle. Although people may be opposed to a more restrictive system of bin collection, they may be even unhappier about increases in their council tax as a result of their local authority having been fined for exceeding its landfill quota. In Document 2, however, there is evidence that an AWC scheme is not a necessary condition for having a good recycling record, nor is it a sufficient condition since some local authorities send a great deal of refuse to landfill sites despite having an AWC system. Nevertheless, Document 3 provides evidence that there is a strong correlation between AWC schemes and good recycling rates. Therefore, AWC schemes could prevent steep increases in council tax that would be more unpopular than the new refuse collection systems.

The utilitarian principle is that we should act in such a way that would result in the greatest happiness of the greatest number. In order to apply this principle, a happiness calculation has to be performed. If an AWC system could prevent major increases in council tax (for the reasons given above), then many people may be happy because they would have more of their own money to spend. However, a minority may be unhappy, for example the people who live in blocks of flats (described in Document 1) who may suffer from smells and even health risks from communal bins, especially in hot weather. A major criticism of the utilitarian principle would be that the interests of such a minority could be disregarded in order to concentrate on what benefits the greatest number. Nevertheless, it could be possible to help people who live in blocks of flats either by having special weekly collections of food waste for this type of housing or, better still, by providing education about how to dispose of food waste (as advocated in Document 1).

Another problem with utilitarianism is that when we talk about 'the greatest number', we usually mean human beings who are alive now, and we could forget about our responsibilities to future generations who may suffer if we do not consider the protection of the environment. Principles of environmentalism advocate care for the planet, especially in respect of preventing or minimising the effects of global warming. Failure to care for the environment could be said to be immoral because of the impact of climate change on future human beings; recycling can be an important way of reducing the environmental impact of sending waste to landfill. Document 4 shows that Britain has a bad record on dumping rubbish in landfill, and environmentalists would argue that we have a clear duty to increase recycling rates for the sake of future generations.

Cynics may suggest that, if local authorities are prevented from using landfill, they will incinerate instead, and incineration has its own environmental problems. However, AWC schemes can encourage recycling, as Document 3 suggests, by requiring householders to separate refuse. With refuse separated appropriately, local authorities should be able to develop effective recycling systems that could help reduce carbon emissions.

Therefore, the democratic principle has to be treated with care because we have yet to see the effect on public opinion of penalty charges for those local authorities that do not increase their recycling rates. The utilitarian principle is also limited in its effectiveness because it would appear to disregard the interests of the minority who live in apartment blocks and those of future generations who may suffer from the effects of global

warming. The environmentalist principle could be seen as strong because it does seem, from the evidence in the resource booklet, that there is a correlation between recycling rates and AWC systems.

Given the evidence that Britain has a particularly bad recycling record, and given the likelihood that penalty charges for exceeding landfill quota will lead to steep increases in council tax, local authorities are right to introduce AWC schemes.

The argument begins with a definition of the key term.

> Throughout the answer, there are several references to the evidence in the resource booklet and this evidence is dealt with critically, rather than being taken at face value. For example, in the second paragraph of the argument, the LGA's findings are questioned.
>
> Several principles are identified and applied. The effectiveness of these principles is then explored, with some shown to be less effective than others.
>
> There is a strong argument for a particular conclusion. Counter-arguments are raised (e.g. paragraph 6) and responded to. There is some hypothetical reasoning (e.g. the third sentence of paragraph 4) and use of intermediate conclusions (e.g. the last sentence of paragraph 3).
>
> The principles used are relevant to this particular issue. Kantianism, human rights, egalitarianism and libertarianism are not as relevant — but note that these may be useful in dealing with other issues that may appear in Unit F503 papers.
>
> There is a clear conclusion to this argument, which is that AWC systems should be implemented.
>
> It is also possible to write a strong argument advocating their abolition. Local authorities may protest that AWC systems are not 'fortnightly', but it is clear that there has been a considerable reduction in the quality of service over the years while, at the same time, council tax has risen significantly. Just because it is possible that food waste can be wrapped properly, it does not necessarily follow that it *will* be, and does global warming not mean that rubbish should be collected *more* frequently? Is it not a false dilemma to suggest that we can have weekly rubbish collections *or* good recycling rates, when the evidence from other countries (Document 2) is that it is possible to have both? If local authorities do not send waste to landfill, it does not necessarily follow that they recycle more. If people do not have all their waste collected weekly, will there be an increase in fly tipping? Do recycling schemes necessarily help the environment? How many people produce carbon emissions by driving to municipal tips or bottle banks?

■ ■ ■

C-grade answer

Dilemma: 'Should councils provide weekly collections of all rubbish which could result in EU fines and environmental damage or should they introduce AWC schemes which are unpopular with voters and could lead to poorer living conditions?'

All rubbish should be collected weekly. This is because there are other ways of cutting down the amount of rubbish than collecting it less often. For example Document 2 says that '21 managed recycling levels higher than the 30% average'. Here it is referring to councils still using weekly collection. What this means is that even though they still collect rubbish weekly, the councils are still cutting down on the amount of rubbish without the need for AWC, which means that other ways can work.

However, although other ways work, there is still the call for AWC, encouraged by the statement that the UK is the 'dustbin of Europe' (Document 4). However, even this claim is exaggerated and largely unsupported. The graph shows only 'estimated' figures for the UK, which could be inaccurate. Also, we will produce more rubbish because we have a high population. In the graph, figures should be a percentage. Also, other countries may not be using AWC and may be getting rid of rubbish by incinerating it. All of these reasons show that the statement that the UK is the 'dustbin of Europe' is untrue and that by having weekly collections instead of AWC, we will not necessarily increase our rubbish and reduce our recycling.

There is the principle of libertarianism which says that there should be personal freedom. Why should we reduce our rubbish or store it for two weeks if we do not want to? This idea is one of the main reasons for choosing weekly collections over AWC, as it gives the option to recycle and does not make it compulsory.

There is also the principle of utilitarianism, which is the greatest happiness of the greatest number. In this case, it seems that the greatest number want weekly collections and so surely if this were the case AWC should be stopped.

In conclusion, weekly collections are the better option to choose because both the principles of libertarianism and utilitarianism fit into this argument and because there are other less drastic ways of reducing rubbish and increasing recycling.

The dilemma is well expressed. The candidate explains the harm that could arise from each choice.

The first two paragraphs in the argument are quite strong, since the candidate makes some critical references to the documents in the resource booklet instead of taking the material at face value.

However, the use of ethical principles is fairly weak, and there needs to be more development. Libertarians would find it difficult to argue that AWC is a violation of personal freedoms. Maybe the most libertarian solution would be 'pay as you throw', which would allow those people who choose not to recycle to pay for their usage. Maybe the whole problem is that local government is responsible for rubbish collection rather than private businesses. Perhaps people should be free to choose and pay for their preferred rubbish collection service.

It is also rather simplistic to say that utilitarianism would be opposed to AWC because opinion polls show it to be unpopular. Opinion polls are not a reliable way of calculating what would make people happy. They do not, for example, consider short-term and long-term happiness. People may be opposed to AWC but they may also be opposed to EU fines, tax increases and damage to the environment. If AWC produces its intended effects, it is possible that more happiness would be produced in the long term.

To achieve a higher mark, the candidate needs to identify environmental ethics as a principle, since this issue has significant environmental implications. Do we, for example, have a moral duty to protect the environment for the sake of future generations?

The final conclusion is fairly weak because there is no evaluation of the strengths and weaknesses of the principles. To develop an argument, some of the common criticisms of utilitarianism and libertarianism need to be identified. Because of this lack of evaluation, the reasoning in the candidate's argument is not sophisticated enough to achieve a top-band mark.

Learning and Careers